70

COMMON

BUTTERFLIES

OF THE SOUTHWEST

Richard Bailowitz *and* Douglas Danforth

WESTERN NATIONAL PARKS ASSOCIATION
TUCSON, ARIZONA

The authors would like to thank Steven J. Cary and James P. Brock for their critical review.

Library of Congress Cataloging-in-Publication Data
Bailowitz, Richard A. (Richard Allen)
    70 common butterflies of the Southwest / Richard Bailowitz and Douglas Danforth.
        p.   cm.
    Includes bibliographical references (p.   ) and index.
    ISBN 1–877856–84–3 (pbk.)
    1. Butterflies—Southwestern States.   I. Danforth, Douglas.
II. Title.
QL551.S87B35 1997
595.78'9'0979 — dc21

                                                        97-42153
                                                        CIP

Published by Western National Parks Association

Net proceeds from WNPA publications support educational
and research programs in the National Park Service.

Editorial: Susan Lamb
Production: Laura Symms-Wallace
Book design: Campana Design
Map illustration: Deborah Reade
Cover photograph: Two-tailed swallowtail, Douglas Danforth
All text photography by Douglas Danforth except Tailed copper and
Mead's Wood-nymph by Steven Cary

Printed in China by Imago

INTRODUCTION

*B*utterflies are easily the most noticed, well-liked, colorful, and benign insects. Nearly 400 species occur in the Southwest, more than half the total number in all of North America. The Southwest region covered in this book includes several distinct deserts, all or part of several mountain ranges, forests, chaparral, and grasslands. Rainfall varies considerably across the region, from three inches or less annually in the low deserts to more than thirty inches on some of the higher mountain ranges. Butterfly species align themselves with specific habitats, and so a variety of habitats produces a greater diversity of species. The rich mosaic of habitats in the Southwest is why so many different butterflies make this area their home.

THE LIFE CYCLE OF A BUTTERFLY

A butterfly's life consists of four stages and—except for migratory or influx species—butterflies in one or another of these stages are present all year. Each butterfly begins life as an egg. After several days or more, a caterpillar, also called a *larva*, hatches. The larvae feed on a specific plant and are voracious about their eating. They can eat twice their body weight in a day. Consuming so much food fuels incredible body growth, forcing them to shed several shells of skin. This is called *molting*, and all caterpillars go through about five molts. Each molt gives them a new, oversized skin into which they can grow. After a series of molts, the caterpillar then tries to find a secure hiding spot where it goes through the rest of its metamorphosis. The caterpillar *pupates*, forming a protective envelope known as a *chrysalis*.

The eggs, larvae, and pupae are often invaded by parasitic wasps or flies. However, if all goes well, an adult will be produced. After at least a week, the pupa will split open to allow the adult—the only form of the insect that has wings—to emerge. Initially, the wings are crumpled. But the butterfly pumps a fluid into the pattern of veins on its wings and after about an hour it is ready to fly. Now it goes forth to find a mate, feed on nectar, and (if it is female) lay eggs on its host plant.

After mating, males continue to pursue additional females. Females, on the other hand, usually fly off to find suitable oviposition sites. Chemical and visual cues from the plants determine exactly where the eggs will be deposited. An individual female can lay as many as several hundred eggs. Females are usually larger than males, since when gravid they have a heavier abdomen to lift into the air.

If a butterfly's flight is listed as "July to August," it means the adults copulate and lay eggs during those months. Their eggs or caterpillars must survive winter and the following spring and pupate in time for the next generation of adults to be ready for flight in July and August. Individuals at lower elevations tend to fly earlier in the spring than their high-altitude counterparts in order to take advantage of a time when young leaves or fresh flowers are available.

In the low, warm deserts, some species are always breeding and you can find their adults flying year-round even though any single individual may be flying for only a week or two. Where the growing season is short, the flight periods of butterflies are also short. Some species are single-brooded and fairly well synchronized so that all of the adults are on the wing at approximately the same time.

WHERE TO FIND BUTTERFLIES

Butterflies are everywhere, in cities and wilderness areas from the lowest, driest, hottest deserts to far above timberline on the cold, wind-swept slopes of the Rocky Mountains. The key to finding them is to explore and experiment. Look for butterflies at different times of day—from early morning to dusk— and in different weather conditions, such as after rains. In the Southwest, peak butterfly-watching season is considered to be July through September.

Find sites where male butterflies are seeking mates. Most male butterflies use one of three means to locate females: perching on hilltops, patrolling

gullies, or perching on trees or shrubs. Many butterfly species are sexually *dimorphic*, meaning that females have a different color or pattern than males.

When looking for a particular butterfly, seek out its larval food, or host plant. Caterpillars feed on relatively few plant species, while most adults feed on many different flowering plants. If you find the larval food source, such as the popular Wright's buckwheat, you'll likely find butterflies like acmon blues or Mormon metalmarks, provided your timing is right. Or, if you are around oaks, you may find California sisters and duskywings.

Your chances of finding butterflies increase if you find an area where two different habitats overlap, because there will likely be more variety of host plants there. Search openings in the forests where canyons cut through piñons and junipers, or where grasslands border riparian zones, or in desert arroyos.

ATTRACTING
BUTTERFLIES
TO YOUR GARDEN

Butterflies enjoy a large variety of flowers. Some flowers attract butterflies more than others, and it depends upon their size, shape, depth, color, and nectar production. In city gardens, verbenas, lantanas, rosemary, salvias, mints, Jupiter's beard, and composites have high success rates. A gardener may find it helpful to wander through local plant nurseries observing which plants attract butterflies. In the wild, members of the mustard, pea, and composite families are usually winners. Several species of groundsel, sweetbush, buckbrush, seepwillow, desert broom, and rabbitbrush are usually popular nectar sources. Because populations of both insects and flowers fluctuate from year to year, your success in finding butterflies will vary as well.

Finding water is another trick for locating butterflies, especially in areas of low rainfall. Not all butterflies visit flowers; most need to hydrate themselves, replacing vital trace elements. Puddles in canyons, intermittent creeks, and *tinajas* (depressions where water collects after rainfall) attract more butterflies than do the edges of fast-moving mountain streams. When humidity is high during the summer rainy season, large numbers of one or a few species may gather for a "puddle party," mingling at a single wet spot.

HOW TO USE THIS BOOK

Lepidopterists organize butterflies into families, but various authorities may group or split butterfly species into families somewhat differently. We have chosen a conservative approach and limited the butterflies in this book to just seven families: swallowtails (*Papilionidae*), whites and sulfurs (*Pieridae*), gossamer wings (*Lycaenidae*), metalmarks (*Riodinidae*), snout butterflies (*Libytheidae*), brush-footed butterflies (*Nymphalidae*), and skippers (*Hesperiidae*). With each species, we list its common name followed by its scientific name. These are the official names used by the North American Butterfly Association (NABA).

Each butterfly species has a distinct range. Although some species are generalists and may be seen throughout the region, others are limited to a certain plant or group of plants upon which their caterpillars feed. When a butterfly occurs in different forms in different parts of its range, these variants are called subspecies. As a rule, higher altitude specimens are darker than those from the lowlands.

A butterfly's size is measured in inches, from forewing tip to forewing tip in "standard position," which is measured with the front wings pulled forward so that their hind edges are straight across, perpendicular to the line of the body. Although this position is unnatural, it maximizes the amount of wing surface visible and standardizes size descriptions.

SWALLOWTAIL FAMILY
(Papilionidae)

PIPEVINE SWALLOWTAIL

SWALLOWTAILS NUMBER OVER 500 SPECIES AROUND THE WORLD and include the largest butterflies known. They are quite noticeable because of their size and greatly admired for their beauty. Most of the dozen or so species in the Southwest have elegantly elongated tips on their hind wings that resemble the tails of swallows, hence the family name.

Swallowtail caterpillars have a foul-smelling, forked gland behind the head called an *osmeterium*. It is usually hidden but can be everted to deter predators.

All swallowtails visit flowers, fluttering their wings while feeding. Swallowtails are large and heavy-bodied, and it may be that this fluttering keeps their weight from breaking off the heads of the flowers, or perhaps it is just for balance.

1 · Pipevine Swallowtail
Battus philenor

Pipevine swallowtails frequent a variety of flowers in deserts and foothills as well as verbenas and lantanas in city gardens. Often, they are one of the first butterflies seen on summer mornings, either in flight or basking with wings open to the sun's warmth. On hot days, adults visit puddles and damp spots.

Their ornate, reddish larvae feed avidly on pipevine leaves, ingesting aristolochic acids that make them and their adults unpalatable. Several other species, such as the red-spotted purple, mimic the appearance of poisonous pipevine adults to avoid being eaten. Species distasteful to birds and other predators often are brightly colored to advertise that they are poisonous.

RANGE	In open areas throughout the region, most commonly to the south.
SIZE	2.5 to 3.25 inches.
HOST PLANTS	Pipevines.
FLIGHT	April to October northward, year-round in the south.

2 · Two-Tailed Swallowtail
Papilio (Pterourus) multicaudatus

RANGE	Most of the Southwest, except in the lowest deserts.
SIZE	3.5 to 4.5 inches.
HOST PLANTS	Various plants, including wild cherry and ash.
FLIGHT	March to October.

This swallowtail favors canyons. Hikers cannot help but notice its large, yellow and black wings should it glide by them. Although the two-tailed swallowtail is a powerful flyer, it is relatively easy to approach at damp spots or while it feeds on nectar.

As is common with many butterflies, spring adults are smaller than adults during other times of the year. The two tails on each hind wing identify this species; western tiger swallowtails (*Papilio rutulus*) of northern Arizona and New Mexico have only one tail on each hind wing.

3 · Black Swallowtail
Papilio polyxenes coloro

This species has two forms in the Southwest: adults in southern California and western Arizona deserts are mostly yellow—belying the name black swallowtail—while from the mountains of central Arizona south through western Texas they are mostly black with a double row of yellow-orange spots across both sets of wings.

To deter hungry birds, adults resemble unpleasant-tasting pipevine swallowtails. Males are strong hilltoppers and it is not unusual to climb small hills in the spring and find several males perched on low vegetation at the summit. The caterpillars (known by gardeners as parsley worms) are green with yellow-spotted black rings circling the body.

RANGE	Throughout the Southwest.
SIZE	2.5 to 3.5 inches.
HOST PLANTS	Leaves and flower heads of the carrot family such as garden parsley, dill, and fennel; also the citrus family.
FLIGHT	March to October.

4 · Giant Swallowtail
Papilio (Heraclides) cresphontes

Giant swallowtails are common garden visitors in low desert cities such as El Centro, Yuma, and Phoenix. They are usually near the citrus trees that host "orange dogs," a common name for their caterpillars, which look like moving bird droppings. Their chrysalids are shades of tan, brown, and green, blending with the leaves and stems of citrus trees.

Giant swallowtails are, as the name suggests, quite large in wingspan. Adults are fond of lantana flowers and zinnias, both common in city gardens.

RANGE	Commonly in west, less commonly northward and eastward.
SIZE	3.5 to 4 inches.
HOST PLANTS	Hop tree, prickly ash, star leaf, and citrus trees.
FLIGHT	March to November.

WHITES & SULFURS FAMILY
(Pieridae)

SOUTHERN DOGFACE

OUT OF APPROXIMATELY ELEVEN HUNDRED SPECIES IN THIS
family worldwide, nearly three dozen occur in the Southwest. They are abundant
butterflies, often appearing earlier in the year than members of other families.

As their name implies, most of them are shades of white, yellow, or even orange.
Along with their particular pattern of wing *venation*, whites and sulfurs possess six
full-sized legs, each with forked claws. Many species travel seasonally and are strong,
continuous fliers that seldom glide. Some also have different-looking adults at different times of the year, apparently keyed to the amount of daylight. All species
within this family visit flowers.

5 · Checkered White *Pieris (Pontia) protodice*

From middle elevations in the mountains down into the deserts, this is one of our most common insects. Particularly noteworthy for its ability to withstand prolonged high temperatures, checkered whites are still fluttering about in open country even in mid-June when other butterflies are long gone because of the unrelenting heat. They spend their winters in the pupal stage.

Females are usually patterned with more of the characteristic rectangular, charcoal-colored spots than are males. Adults in flight during the spring are more heavily marked than those later in the year.

These butterflies see ultraviolet light. They reflect patterns invisible to our human eyes but which aid in their identifying the opposite sex.

RANGE	Open spaces throughout the region, especially in low country and disturbed areas.
SIZE	1.5 inches.
HOST PLANTS	Wild mustards and capers such as beeplant.
FLIGHT	Whenever weather permits, year-round in the deserts.

6 · Cabbage White *Pieris (Artogeia) rapae*

Since its introduction into North America in the mid-nineteenth century, the cabbage white has spread coast to coast. It is very common in southwestern towns and cities and occasionally forms colonies along watercourses away from population centers.

Cabbage whites usually spend colder periods in the pupal stage. Their caterpillars eat cabbage leaves (hence the name) and related plants. If there is a large enough number, they can damage crops.

The males have one black spot on the upper surface of their fore wings, the females have two, and the wing tips of both appear to have been dipped in ink. A creamy yellow color shows when their wings are held together in repose.

RANGE	In discrete colonies throughout the region.
SIZE	1.4 to 1.6 inches.
HOST PLANTS	Cabbage leaves in gardens, watercress and other mustards in the wild.
FLIGHT	April to October in the high country, year-round at lower elevations.

7 · Pearly Marble *Euchloe hyantis*

This beautiful species is one of the first signs of spring. Males patrol hilltops for females, revealing their luscious, green-patterned undersides whenever they perch. Since this species is not very tame, however, a pair of close-focusing binoculars will come in handy to see this pattern.

Many species of butterflies bask in the sun to raise their body temperatures high enough so that they can fly. While most open their wings for the sun to warm the upper surface, several species including the pearly marble close their wings, turning them sideways so the sun can warm the underside.

RANGE	Middle elevations, central New Mexico west to the Mojave Desert, avoids low desert country.
SIZE	1.0 to 1.2 inches.
HOST PLANTS	A variety of wild mustards.
FLIGHT	February to May, depending upon elevation.

8 · Sara Orangetip *Anthocharis sara*

This early spring flier graces the deserts and mountains with a frail dignity, delicate flight, and crisp pattern. As the name suggests, the white fore wings are tipped with glowing orange, evident even in flight.

Lingering looks at this beauty are rare, for it usually perches only for short periods. Sara orangetips are fond of manzanita flowers in canyons and open country.

Another species, the desert orangetip (*Anthocharis cethura*), is confined to elevations below 4,500 feet. It has a yellow base color (white in southeastern California) and a green rather than gray underside pattern. Desert orangetip males are strong hilltoppers, but Sara orangetip males patrol valleys looking for mates.

RANGE	Extreme west Texas, westward throughout the region.
SIZE	1.0 to 1.3 inches.
HOST PLANTS	A variety of wild mustards.
FLIGHT	January to May, depending upon elevation.

9 · Orange Sulfur *Colias eurytheme*

On warm days around alfalfa fields, you are likely to see streams of orange sulfurs in various shades of white, yellow, and orange. Enormous numbers breed in alfalfa, their larvae's favorite food plant. They will eat any of several legumes, however, and may be found from mountains to deserts.

Adults rarely display their wings' upper surfaces because as soon as they land, they close their wings. There is a solid black border around the wings of males, but orange spots interrupt females' wing borders. Some females are pale greenish-white in color.

Orange sulfurs occasionally hybridize with a similar species, clouded sulfurs (*Colias philodice*), which look identical but tend to be more yellow than orange. Clouded sulfurs do not reflect ultraviolet light patterns like orange sulfurs.

RANGE	Throughout the Southwest.
SIZE	1.4 to 1.7 inches.
HOST PLANTS	Alfalfa, clover, other legumes.
FLIGHT	February to November in the high country, year-round in the deserts.

10 · Southern Dogface *Colias (Zerene) cesonia*

No butterfly could be more aptly named —a glimpse at the poodle-head pattern on its front wings is sure to bring a chuckle to anyone. The pattern is visible only if the insect is backlit, since it virtually never perches with parted wings. Females lack crispness in the dogface pattern but have characteristically *falcate* (sickle-shaped) fore wings.

Southern dogfaces are strong fliers and frequently gather with other sulfurs at puddle parties to gather water and trace minerals used in the production of pheromones. It is easy to approach adults as they are nectaring at a variety of flowers, such as rabbitbrush and salvia.

RANGE	Commonly throughout the Southwest in cities, deserts, foothills, and mountains.
SIZE	1.6 to 2.0 inches.
HOST PLANTS	False indigo and other legumes.
FLIGHT	Mostly warm weather, but occasionally through the winter.

11 · Cloudless Sulfur *Phoebis sennae*

During summer monsoons and occasional springs, large numbers of this mostly Mexican species migrate northward into the Southwest. This influx may be so strong that several can pass over a given location every minute, pausing only at damp spots and nectar before moving northward again. They establish temporary colonies where larval food plants are available, only to be wiped out by freezing temperatures in winter.

Though not true southwestern residents, cloudless sulfurs in their seasonal abundance are hard to miss. Males are immaculate, bright lemon-yellow; females are pale orange to greenish-white. If disturbed while copulating, they may take flight without disengaging, the male flying with the female hanging underneath.

RANGE	Mostly the southern half of the region, straying northward.
SIZE	1.9 to 2.3 inches.
HOST PLANTS	Various sennas.
FLIGHT	Nearly year-round but mostly July to October.

12 · Mexican Yellow *Eurema mexicanum*

This familiar, slow-flying resident of the southern Southwest increases in abundance with the season, often pushing northward to include the entire Southwest by late summer. Mexican yellows are as comfortable in open deserts as they are in coniferous forest clearings. In warm seasons, they are found beneath the forest canopy, as well as in the open on flowers and damp soil, and commonly form puddle parties.

Males are somewhat brighter than females, and the size and shape of the hind wing tail varies with the season. Adults nectar at a variety of flowers, such as Arizona trumpet.

RANGE	Resident in southern half, irregular northward.
SIZE	1.4 to 1.7 inches.
HOST PLANTS	Various legumes, such as white-ball acacia.
FLIGHT	Year-round in the deserts, April to October northward.

13 · Sleepy Orange *Eurema nicippe*

A medium-sized, cheddar cheese–colored butterfly spotted in a city garden is probably a sleepy orange. It perches with wings closed, revealing a pale orange underside laced with reddish lines. Sleepy orange adults feed avidly at flowers, especially red ones such as salvia and cardinal flower.

On sweltering summer days, they form puddle parties in foothill canyons. They can tolerate moderate freezes and fly throughout desert winters. The tailed orange (*Eurema proterpia*) is similar except its veins are outlined in black and it lacks most of the wide black wing borders. It occurs in southern Arizona and New Mexico but cannot survive winters there, requiring Mexican stock to replenish its population each season.

RANGE	Throughout the region, more commonly southward.
SIZE	1.3 to 1.7 inches.
HOST PLANTS	Senna.
FLIGHT	Most common in late summer, year-round in the deserts.

14 · Dainty Sulfur *Nathalis iole*

It is easy to miss the dainty sulfur, the smallest of yellow butterflies, which seldom bares its lovely, yellow-and black wing surface. Except in summer, dainty sulfurs fly close to the ground for reflected warmth. Their low flight, small size, and pale greenish-yellow underside blend with the rocks on which they perch, making them less vulnerable to predators.

From high mountain meadows to desert pavement, all habitats support dainty sulfurs, but they survive winter only on the region's southern edge and are not regular farther north until summer.

RANGE	Throughout the region.
SIZE	.9 to 1.0 inch.
HOST PLANTS	Small, herb composites such as golden fleece.
FLIGHT	Year-round.

GOSSAMER WING FAMILY
(Lycaenidae)

JUNIPER HAIRSTREAK

BUTTERFLIES IN THIS FAMILY ARE SMALL TO VERY SMALL IN SIZE, IN various shades of blue, orange, and brown. Some are extremely brilliant in color with wing scales that are complex in shape, resulting in different colors or iridescence depending upon how light bounces off them.

All gossamer wing butterflies have eyes that are notched around the antennae, instead of spherical or nearly so. The males of this family have somewhat reduced front legs without claws, while the females' legs are more normal.

There are more than forty-five hundred species of gossamer wings throughout the world, with at least sixty-five species reported from the American Southwest. The family is broken into several subfamilies. One subfamily, the coppers, are named for their coloration. Another group, the hairstreaks, have wispy tails. When perched they keep their wings closed and constantly rub their tails back and forth as a way of distracting predators from attacking their vital ends. A third group, the blues, tend to be small with various shades of pale blue on their upper surfaces.

15 · Tailed Copper *Lycaena arota*

Found in coniferous forest clearings, the tailed copper is the most common and generally distributed of a handful of species of coppers recorded from the Southwest. The undersides of its wings are highly patterned, unlike most other coppers. Purple iridescence glazes the lustrous copper of males, while females are a mix of brown and orange.

Named for its tailed hind wing, it shares this characteristic with only one other species of copper found in San Diego, California. Tailed copper males perch on small bushes in clearings, usually in the morning, to await passing females.

RANGE	Central New Mexico and northern Arizona, northward.
SIZE	.9 to 1.1 inches.
HOST PLANTS	Currants and gooseberries.
FLIGHT	July to August.

16 · Great Blue Hairstreak *Atlides halesus*

The iridescent turquoise color of this species must be seen to be believed. However, since hairstreaks generally perch with their wings together, the glint of its blue can only be seen when it flies. One usually sees it as a triangular-shaped, mostly black butterfly with two long, twisted, thread-like tails on its hind wings.

Great blues favor tall flowering shrubs or vines and often nectar upon seep willow. They are a solitary species, quite fond of damp spots. In the afternoon, males frequent treetops on the summits of hills. Even if disturbed, the great blue will often return repeatedly to its treetop territory.

RANGE	Throughout the region.
SIZE	1.2 to 1.5 inches.
HOST PLANTS	Flowers and leaves of mistletoe.
FLIGHT	Mostly March to October.

17 · Leda Ministreak *Ministrymon leda*

RANGE	Spottily throughout the region.
SIZE	.7 inch.
HOST PLANTS	Predominately mesquite.
FLIGHT	April to October.

On a hot summer's day, the shady side of a broad-leafed shrub may be filled with dozens of this little species. Their scissoring wings may reveal a glimpse of the upper wings' coloration. Leda ministreaks are most conspicuous by their numbers. There are two distinct seasonal forms of this species: the short day-length form, *ines*, has more powder blue on its upper surface and more of a two-toned underside than the long day-length form, *leda*.

Adults visit a variety of flowers such as desert broom. Due to the comparatively muscular construction of the thorax in small hairstreaks such as the Leda ministreak, their flight is extremely rapid, erratic, and difficult to follow.

18 · Juniper Hairstreak *Mitoura grynea siva*

This beautiful species is a possibility wherever junipers are found, most commonly within the piñon/juniper belt between 4,000 and 7,000 feet. It is quite regular at flowers and damp soil, but some naturalists will tap on juniper trees to find resting adults.

Fresh specimens newly emerged from the chrysalis are brown to red-brown on the upper surface but emerald green below, crossed by a zigzag white line. The green is very evident when the juniper hairstreak is taking nectar, for example, atop a mala mujer or seep willow. Juniper hairstreaks have a rapid flight when disturbed, but they often return to the same perch, and thus are fairly easy to observe.

RANGE	Throughout most of the region, avoids lowest deserts.
SIZE	.8 to .9 inch.
HOST PLANTS	Junipers.
FLIGHT	March to September.

19 · Gray Hairstreak *Strymon melinus*

Although never abundant, this species is the most common and widespread of the hairstreaks. Its larvae feed on a broad array of plants, which is quite uncommon for caterpillars.

Gray hairstreaks bask in the early morning light and open their wings to gain warmth. While basking, they expose their mouse-gray upper surface, which is broken by a pronounced black-centered red area at the base of their tails. Such a pattern clearly identifies this species. The males can be distinguished from females by their orange abdomens.

RANGE	Throughout the region.
SIZE	.8 to 1.0 inch.
HOST PLANTS	A wide range of food plants in many families.
FLIGHT	February to November.

20 · Arizona Hairstreak *Erora quaderna*

Arizona hairstreaks are a subtle jewel of the butterfly world, a specialty of the Southwest. While males are dark above, the upper surface of females is iridescent blue on black. The underside of both males and females is pale emerald green marked with small spots of red, and the fringes are orange. Unlike other hairstreaks, this species usually lacks tails.

Despite its wealth of color, the Arizona hairstreak's small size and stillness while perched make it quite cryptic on a flower such as buckbrush. Males love to perch on hilltop trees, where they can be enticed to reveal themselves with a tap or a toss of a stick. Both sexes of this species avidly visit damp spots.

RANGE	Central Arizona and New Mexico through west Texas, especially in mountain oaks.
SIZE	.7 to .8 inch.
HOST PLANTS	Unknown.
FLIGHT	Mostly March to May, also in July.

21 · Western Pygmy-Blue *Brephidium exile*

When its shadow can be more evident than the creature itself, a butterfly must indeed be small. This species is generally considered the smallest of North American butterflies, although two or three others come close.

Pygmies are denizens of open flatlands, disturbed areas, and the dry benches above watercourses. They can be quite common in these wastelands where few other species are at home, buzzing like gnats around saltbush and taking nectar from flowers such as pepper grass. In spite of its miniscule size, the species is known to wander considerable distances from its breeding grounds.

RANGE	Lowlands throughout the region.
SIZE	.5 to .6 inch.
HOST PLANTS	Leaves, flowers, and fruits of the goosefoot family, both native and introduced.
FLIGHT	Year-round in the deserts, warm seasons elsewhere.

22 · Marine Blue *Leptotes marina*

When a flight of marine blues hits stride, they can be so abundant that they over-shadow other types of butterflies. Because male are mostly blue and females mostly brown, they may appear to be two different

species, but their zebra-striped undersides of dark and light bluish-gray mark them both as marine blues.

They are most abundant at middle elevations below 6,000 feet. On hot days, males frequent damp spots in canyons, wet areas around swimming pools, and freshly watered gardens. Marine blues are capable of rapid flight, unlike many other blues.

RANGE	Highest peaks to lowest deserts throughout the region, more common southward.
SIZE	.7 to .9 inch.
HOST PLANTS	Flowers and fruits of various legumes.
FLIGHT	Summer in the high country, year-round in the deserts.

23 · Reakirt's Blue *Hemiargus isola*

Reakirt's blue is another widespread, small blue butterfly, common in yards and gardens as well as in abandoned fields, deserts, grasslands, and clearings in coniferous forests. The upper surface is blue in males, and blue and brown in females. The underside of the fore wing has a string of large, black spots ringed with white, which helps separate Reakirt's blue from other blues.

They are common visitors to puddles and, at times, gather at the water's edge in large numbers. By the end of summer, wandering adults establish colonies far north of their permanent range.

RANGE	Throughout the region.
SIZE	.7 to .8 inch.
HOST PLANTS	Flowers and young leaves of many species of legumes, both herbs and shrubs.
FLIGHT	March to November.

24 · Spring Azure *Celestrina argiolus*

This cosmopolitan species varies its choice of habitats, food plants, flight periods, and even its appearance. This suggests to some researchers that more than one species may be involved in a species-complex that includes the spring azure. Generally, the spring azure is larger and brighter than many other blues.

Common in deserts in spring, it flies year-round in foothills and lower mountain canyons. Puddle parties of spring azure males are beacons of light along streamsides, erupting in a cloud of blue if disturbed. Females have wide brown borders and their blue is less brilliant.

RANGE	Throughout most of the region, more commonly northward.
SIZE	.7 to 1.0 inch.
HOST PLANTS	A wide array of plants.
FLIGHT	Year-round, except at high altitude.

25 · Silvery Blue *Glaucopsyche lygdamus*

RANGE	A Rocky Mountain species occurring southward into the Southwest.
SIZE	.9 to 1.1 inches.
HOST PLANTS	Any of several legumes.
FLIGHT	May to August.

Silvery blue males are the brightest of all the blues, even the spring azures, although the females are not as bright. Since silvery blues often fly in company with other species of blues, it is a challenge for the naturalist to identify them.

Several forms or subspecies occur across the Southwest, differing slightly in hue or size of spotting. The brilliance of the upper surface is contrasted by the pure gray underside, broken only by a few large black spots ringed with white. Adults are very fond of iris and astragalus flowers.

26 · Acmon Blue *Plebejus acmon*

Acmon blues are the most common of several species of blues that have a row of tiny orange crescents, called *lunules*, along the edge of the hind wings (either on the underside or on both surfaces of the wings). Both sexes of acmon blues possess orange lunules on both wing surfaces, but the base color of males is blue, in females gray-brown.

This species is especially attracted to damp spots. Like other blues, acmons are prone to cycles of abundance and fly almost any time of the year in the deserts. They are confined to summer months in the cooler parts of the Southwest. The orange-bordered blue (*Plebejus melissa*), a similar species that also has orange markings on its front wings, frequents sagebrush deserts and clearings in piñon/juniper and pine forests.

RANGE	Throughout the Southwest except in the hottest deserts.
SIZE	.7 to .8 inch.
HOST PLANTS	Some populations feed on legumes; others prefer buckwheat.
FLIGHT	Mostly February to October.

METALMARK FAMILY
(Riodinidae)

MORMON METALMARK

ABOUT FIFTEEN HUNDRED SPECIES OF METALMARKS OCCUR worldwide, with South and Central America being especially rich in diversity. Although the Southwest is home to only about ten species of metalmarks, some of them can be locally abundant.

The shape of the wings and the variety of colors in this butterfly family vary so widely that it is difficult to generalize about it. However, metalmarks have long antennae and usually metallic silver or gold spotting somewhere on the wings. Some are tailed like miniature swallowtails while others are iridescent blue like gossamer wing butterflies. Some are orange and black like the brush-foots; some are pale brown like satyrs or skippers.

Metalmarks are grouped together because of their anatomical similarities including leg structure, wing venation, and, especially, the characteritics of their caterpillars. A number of metalmark caterpillars have "honey" glands to attract ants that serve as protective guards in return for honey. Although gossamer wing caterpillars also have these glands, they are in a different location.

27 · Fatal Metalmark *Calephelis nemesis*

RANGE	Across the southern half of the region.
SIZE	.6 to .7 inch.
HOST PLANTS	Seep willow.
FLIGHT	Usually February to October.

Fatal metalmarks have a clear orange undersurface riddled with metallic spotting and a medium brown upper side with darker brown running midway across all wings. They often alight on flowers close to the ground and perch with their wings mostly to completely open. Like many other metalmarks, they also often land on the underside of leaves and seem to disappear.

The species is usually quite tame and does not range far when disturbed, finding a streamside perch or flower head nearby. Most populations of fatal metalmarks are along major river valleys.

28 · Mormon Metalmark *Apodemia mormo*

Mormon metalmarks exemplify the close ties between insect and plant. Their caterpillars feed only on various buckwheat species. Their adults stay fairly true to buckwheat flowers, but have difficulty resisting the flowers of sweetbush and seep willow. Through winters or dry spells, the caterpillars are dormant in leaf litter beneath plants, within plant stems, or in seed heads.

Mormon metalmark adults are highly variable in color even within the same population. On flowers and at hilltops, they perch most often with wings half open, slowly fanning them with a jerky motion unique to the species. As with most metalmarks in the Southwest, this species is very tame, allowing close approach by the interested observer.

RANGE	Throughout the region.
SIZE	.8 to 1.2 inches.
HOST PLANTS	Various buckwheat species.
FLIGHT	Late summer in the north, March to October southward.

SNOUT BUTTERFLY FAMILY
(*Libytheidae*)

AMERICAN SNOUT

OF ALL THE BUTTERFLY FAMILIES, THIS ONE HAS THE FEWEST members. Approximately eight species occur worldwide, with just one in the Southwest. As their name suggests, the family's distinguishing feature is the snout, which consists of elongated *palpi*. These palpi are present in all butterflies and aid in the sense of smell, among other things, but in snout butterflies the palpi are much enlarged, about half as long as the antennae.

The family is also characterized by square-tipped wings and the males have reduced, less functional front legs. Adults rest with wings together but bask with wings apart to regulate their temperature.

29 · American Snout
Libytheana carinenta

Vast migrations of American snouts are common. Often unidirectional from the south, they can be heavy enough to clog car radiators. When such numbers of insects are flying around, it is hard not to take notice.

Snouts readily imbibe nectar from flowers such as desert broom and seep willow and also perch on twigs with their bodies parallel to the branch. Scientists believe a major function of the snout butterfly's enlarged palpi is camouflage: the lowered antennae alongside the palpi resemble a leaf stem, while the mottled underside of the perching adult's wings looks much like a dried leaf. The snout butterfly seems to vary its flight behavior so that it can be mistaken for various other species when on the wing.

RANGE	Throughout the region, most commonly southward.
SIZE	1.3 to 1.6 inches.
HOST PLANTS	Hackberry, several species of which are common in the region.
FLIGHT	Warm weather, most common in the summer.

BRUSH-FOOT FAMILY
(Nymphalidae)

COMMON BUCKEYE

THIS LARGE FAMILY CONSISTS OF MORE THAN 4,000 SPECIES worldwide, with nearly 100 species found in the Southwest alone. Some species live for many months as adults. A number of species are mimics while others use deceptive coloration, pronounced eyespots on their wings, and camouflage to protect themselves.

They use only their four hind legs for walking. They are called "brush-foot" because their front legs are half the size of the other four legs, are covered with hairs, and resemble small brushes. These reduced front legs are loaded with scent receptors used to recognize food plants.

Some of the subgroups of this family—milkweed butterflies and satyrs—have been considered full families in their own right at various times.

30 · Gulf Fritillary
Agraulis vanillae

This is a fairly large and gaudy, commonly noticed species with a strong flight that sometimes carries it far from its normal haunts. Its spectacular underside of large, silvered spots on a tan and red-orange background can bring a gasp to the uninitiated.

The gulf fritillary belongs to a group of brush-foot butterflies known as longwings. Female longwings have "stink clubs" on either side of their abdomens, which disperse pheromones to attract males. The male transfers his own chemical onto these stink clubs to repel other males and maximize his own offsprings' success.

RANGE	Lowlands—especially cities and towns—throughout the region.
SIZE	2.3 to 2.6 inches, occasional dwarves.
HOST PLANTS	Ornamental passionvines in city gardens and native passionvines in canyons.
FLIGHT	Often year-round.

31 · Variegated Fritillary
Euptoieta claudia

RANGE	Throughout the region, less commonly northwestward.
SIZE	1.4 to 2.0 inches, occasionally even smaller.
HOST PLANTS	Plants of many families.
FLIGHT	Year-round, most commonly March through October.

Equally at home in deserts and mountain meadows, this species favors middle elevation grasslands where it can be abundant. There are permanent populations of variegated fritillaries in southern parts of the Southwest, but the species pushes northward each year as far as southern Canada.

In season, females hover slowly over grass tops in search of egg-laying sites, while males hover slowly in search of females. Adult variegated fritillaries can tolerate light frosts and are prone to great variation in size.

32 · Atlantis Fritillary
Speyeria atlantis

This large species has a showy, powerful presence in the high canyons and cienegas of the northern mountains where it alights on damp soil and clusters on a variety of flowers.

Easily the most common and widespread fritillary in the Southwest, it has a strong, direct flight but generally perches with its wings together, revealing a beautiful underside of large silvered spots on a chestnut background. Males of atlantis have *androconia*, or sex scaling, along the wing veins to aid in courtship.

RANGE	Much of the northern two thirds of Arizona and New Mexico.
SIZE	2.0 to 2.4 inches.
HOST PLANTS	Violets.
FLIGHT	June to August.

33 · Arachne Checkerspot *Poladryas arachne*

Arachnes of the lowlands and in the east are pale while those at higher altitudes and in the north are darker. All have black dashes across the middle row of white spots on the underside of their hind wings. Most Arachne checkerspots occur at middle elevations on limestone hills, in pine/oak grassland, or in open pine woodland; a few range down into the Sonoran Desert or up into Canadian Zone forests.

Males spend late mornings on ridges and knolls awaiting females, which are larger and rounder winged. Larvae of Arachnes usually winter in their third molt and continue feeding in the spring to become full-grown.

RANGE	From the northern edge of the region south to southeast Arizona and southwest New Mexico.
SIZE	1.0 to 1.3 inches.
HOST PLANTS	Any of several penstemon species, usually those with thin, green leaves.
FLIGHT	Mostly April to September.

34 · Theona Checkerspot *Thessalia theona*

There are many small, orange-and-black butterflies all over the world. This one has a crisp pattern on its underside, with parallel rows of cream and orange highlighted by black lines. It is a common middle-elevation species in the Southwest.

Males share hilltops with a variety of other species searching for mates and take in trace elements at puddles from time to time. Theona checkerspots in the Sierra Madre of Mexico become progressively darker, probably because of increased rainfall.

RANGE	Middle elevations from central Arizona southeastward to west Texas.
SIZE	.9 to 1.2 inches.
HOST PLANTS	Indian paintbrush.
FLIGHT	Several broods from April to October.

35 · Fulvia Checkerspot
Thessalia fulvia

This widespread species is especially common in New Mexico. Like most checker-spots, it is more easily identified by the pattern on the underside of its wings than by its upper surface. Fulvia checkerspot wings have arguably the simplest pattern, consisting of a solid cream color and simple network of black lines.

The black checkerspot (*Thessalia cyneas*)—a local resident of southeastern Arizona mountains—is closely related enough to resemble fulvias on the underside, but its upperside is nearly black, crossed only by a few red-orange and yellow spots. Its abundance is cyclical, becoming more common after fires.

RANGE	Spottily throughout the region.
SIZE	1.0 to 1.4 inches.
HOST PLANTS	Indian paintbrush.
FLIGHT	Several flights, April to October.

36 · Bordered Patch
Chlosyne lacinia

No species is any more irruptive than the bordered patch. If a visiting female flies through one's yard, she may lay eggs in clusters of 100 or more, usually on the underside of composite leaves. Several weeks later, the yard may be filled with adults. By late summer, this insect is often abundant in city gardens, agricultural fields, deserts, and foothills. It regularly follows the first composites to blossom after a forest fire.

The patterns and coloring of bordered patches vary; the band across their wings may be narrow or wide, and white, yellow, orange, or totally absent. Another species, the California patch (*Chlosyne californica*), occurs in the deserts of southern California and western Arizona. It has a row of orange spots on the edge of the upper side of the hind wings.

RANGE	Throughout the region except the highest peaks.
SIZE	1.1 to 1.6 inches.
HOST PLANTS	Seep willow, goldeneye, sunflowers, and other composites.
FLIGHT	March to October, mostly late summer.

37 · Tiny Checkerspot *Dymasia dymas*

Large numbers of this tiny, dainty, fluttering, orange-and-black butterfly may grace deserts and foothills with their color, especially during summer monsoons. Despite their rapid wing beat, they never seem to get very far, and if the nature-lover follows one for a minute or so, it will surely perch on a twig or flower for easy examination.

A second species, Elada checkerspot (*Texola elada*), often occurs with tiny checker-spots but differs in its less elongated wings, orange-edged underside hind wing, and more intricate pattern underneath. In general, both are sub-tropical species that occur south of an imaginary line from Las Vegas, Nevada to Carlsbad, New Mexico. Their northern limit is set by the length and severity of sub-freezing temperatures.

RANGE	Southern third of the region.
SIZE	.7 to 1.0 inch.
HOST PLANTS	Members of the acanthus family.
FLIGHT	March to October, most commonly in summer.

38 · Texan Crescent *Anthanassa texana*

There are about ten species of crescents in the Southwest, all characterized by a lone, silvery-white crescent near the margin of the underside of the hind wing. Some are wetland species, while others are associated with agricultural fringes. One is likely to come across the Texan crescent in desert arroyos, foothill canyons, pine forest clearings, and especially along major river valleys.

Males patrol for passing females up and down canyons and back and forth across light gaps in riparian areas. Texan crescent adults love shade on hot days and favor flowers of dogbane, buckbrush, and milkweed.

RANGE	Throughout the region, much more common southward.
SIZE	1.1 to 1.4 inches.
HOST PLANTS	*Dicliptera*.
FLIGHT	March to October, sometimes later.

39 · Mylitta Crescent *Phyciodes mylitta*

Mylitta crescents are common from mountain meadows down into foothill canyons. They can be abundant—often nectaring on composites—in the northern halves of New Mexico and Arizona, where males patrol moist canyons.

Males have a black-and-orange upper surface without the cream or yellow typically found on other crescents. Younger caterpillars sometimes roost in silk nests during nonfeeding times to protect themselves from predators.

RANGE	Southern Nevada to east-central New Mexico.
SIZE	1.1 to 1.3 inches.
HOST PLANTS	Thistle leaves.
FLIGHT	March to October.

40 · Field Crescent *Phyciodes campestris*

Field crescents are common roadside butterflies found in western North America from central Mexico into central Alaska. They visit flowers such as dogbane and fleabane. Like other crescents, they are fairly small, mostly orange-and-black, and their flight is rapid and usually low to the ground.

Field crescents favor upland, mountain, and mesa country while painted crescents (*Phyciodes pictus*)—which are darker and have creamy tips under their fore wings—prefer farmlands, marsh edges, and wastelands. Males of both species are smaller and darker than their lighter, larger, more round-winged females.

RANGE	Most of New Mexico and the northern half of Arizona.
SIZE	1.0 to 1.2 inches.
HOST PLANTS	Mostly asters.
FLIGHT	May to September.

41 · Question Mark *Polygonia interrogationis*

Primarily an insect of eastern woodlands, the question mark reaches its westernmost limits in the Southwest. Never found in numbers, it is nonetheless widespread and distinguished by the odd, almost torn look of its wing edges. The brown, black, and white underside of its wings serves to camouflage it on tree bark.

Question marks have a silver question mark on the underside of their hind wings and, occasionally, a pale-violet wing edging.

Especially in the afternoon, males will often find a sunlit spot at the edge of a forest and set up a territory, pugnaciously darting out at intruders while they catch the last of the sun's rays. Adults prefer sap, rotten fruit, excrement, and damp soil.

RANGE	Much of New Mexico, southeastern Arizona, and west Texas.
SIZE	2.0 to 2.3 inches.
HOST PLANTS	Hackberry and elms.
FLIGHT	Mostly late summer and fall.

42 · Satyr Comma *Polygonia satyrus*

Jagged wing edges identify the satyr comma as an anglewing. It is the most common and widespread of four south-western species in this genus. The brightness of its gold, orange, and black upper side, seen when the satyr comma is flying, disappears abruptly when it perches.

Look for it along watercourses in mountains and foothills, especially during cooler weather. It usually avoids flowers, preferring damp soil and decomposing organic matter. It lays its eggs on the underside of leaves, often stacking one upon another. For protection, the larvae will partially cut through the base of a leaf to make its edges droop around them.

RANGE	Widespread but not in the lowest deserts or in west Texas.
SIZE	1.6 to 1.8 inches.
HOST PLANTS	Nettles and willows.
FLIGHT	Several broods, spring through fall.

43 · Mourning Cloak *Nymphalis antiopa*

People out on winter walks may be surprised to see this large, yellow-edged, brown butterfly flutter past. Mourning cloaks winter as adults, taking to the skies on warm days. The territorial males patrol canyons looking for mates and may perch on the ground, a shrub, or even a person.

Adults feed mostly at mud, sap, rotting fruit, and occasionally at willow catkins. Females oviposit clusters of more than 200 eggs. The larvae are gregarious but the adults are generally solitary. Seeing half a dozen mourning cloaks in one day is a lot.

RANGE	Throughout the region, except in the lowest deserts.
SIZE	2.5 to 2.7 inches
HOST PLANTS	Leaves of cottonwoods and willows as well as several plants in other families.
FLIGHT	Year-round, whenever weather permits.

44 · American Lady *Vanessa virginiensis*

The four North American members of the genus *Vanessa* are common residents of the Southwest. All are fair-sized with bright, sometimes gaudy colors, but the identifying mark of an American lady is the presence of two large eyespots on the underside of its hind wings. These eyespots can be seen when it visits flowers, since it commonly perches with wings closed or partly opened.

American ladies are extremely fond of flowers, especially rabbitbrush. Males perch on the ground or high on treetops to wait for passing females as late as 7 p.m. on the summits of hills. In most cases, American ladies pass the winter as adults.

RANGE	Throughout the region.
SIZE	1.5 to 1.7 inches.
HOST PLANTS	Cudweed and related composites.
FLIGHT	March to October, most commonly in late summer.

45 · Painted Lady
Vanessa cardui

RANGE	Throughout the region.
SIZE	1.6 to 2.1 inches.
HOST PLANTS	Numerous species of plants, most of which are composites.
FLIGHT	Warm weather in the mountains, year-round in the deserts.

Present on all major land masses of the world, the painted lady surely earns the title of most widely distributed butterfly on earth. A familiar garden sight, it is also prone to large, unidirectional flights for unexplained reasons. During these flights, usually in the spring, city gardens and mountain canyons alike may teem with adults sipping nectar from flowers.

When their wings are together you can see four small eyespots on the hind wings, which separate painted ladies from American ladies. The west coast lady (*Vanessa annabella*), which is more common to the west, is a brighter orange on its upper side and has an orange (not white) spot on the leading edge of its fore wing.

RANGE	Mountains to deserts, throughout the region.
SIZE	1.6 to 1.8 inches.
HOST PLANTS	Stinging nettles.
FLIGHT	Warm months in the mountains, cool months in the deserts.

The scarlet-on-deep-brown pattern of the upper side of the wings readily separates the red admiral from any other species in the Southwest. It occasionally nectars at flowers such as rosemary and lantana in city gardens and will also feed on sap, excrement, or fermented fruit. However, the red admiral is more common in foothill and mountain riparian areas where it perches on tree trunks and damp soil.

Ordinarily, the rapid flight of red admirals makes them difficult to follow in the air, but they are notably territorial and can be coaxed onto a finger with a bit of patience. In the afternoons, males seek mates on hilltops.

47 · Common Buckeye
Junonia coenia

The delicate, intricate array of red bars and purple-hued eyespots on the upper side of the common buckeye's wings has not yet been put onto fabric, but perhaps it should be. Its large, realistic eyespots may be intended to startle predators when this species opens its wings. The undersides of its wings are tan but infused with reddish overtones during cooler weather.

A number of species that breed throughout the year become rosier during the winter, perhaps in response to shorter days. Oddly, tan individuals tend to be more mobile than reddish ones. Common buckeye males are highly territorial, even pugnacious, in canyons and on dirt roads. Adults take nectar from a variety of flowers such as monkeyflower and seep willow.

RANGE	Open country and middle elevations throughout the region, rarely at high altitude.
SIZE	1.3 to 1.6 inches.
HOST PLANTS	Members of the snapdragon and plantain families.
FLIGHT	Several broods, spring through fall.

48 · Red-Spotted Purple
Basilarchia arthemis

RANGE	Central Arizona and southern New Mexico into west Texas.
SIZE	2.5 to 2.8 inches.
HOST PLANTS	Cottonwoods and willows.
FLIGHT	Several broods, April to October.

Wherever there are willows along watercourses, this iridescent species is likely to perch on branches and dart out lazily at intruders with a characteristic, quick flutter-and-glide flight pattern. Red-spotted purples avoid flowers but come to damp soil, carrion, decaying fruit, or wood, where they may be approached closely.

They are examples of *Batesian mimicry*—a means of protection in which a tasty animal mimics a poisonous one. They resemble pipevine swallowtails, but without tails and with slightly different markings.

Occasional hybrids between red-spotted purples and viceroys reveal a close relationship between them. One subspecies of red-spotted purple along the U.S. border with Canada was considered a different species for many years, until breeding studies confirmed its status as merely a red-spotted purple with a white band down the middle of its wings.

49 · Viceroy
Basilarchia archippus

In much of the country, the viceroy's mimicry of the dark orange-and-black monarch is well known. Monarchs are scarce as breeders in the Southwest, however, and so here the viceroy mimics another distasteful, poisonous species: the queen. Our viceroys have a chocolatey-brown rather than orange background to their black pattern.

In all parts of their range, viceroys can be distinguished from monarchs and queens by their smaller size and by a black line across the hind wings. Viceroys perch on willows above the water along rivers and around ponds and rarely visit flowers, preferring sap and dung instead. Their quick flutter-and-glide flight, typical of the genus, is usually eye-level or higher. The pupae look much like bird droppings.

RANGE	Locally throughout the region, avoiding the higher mountains.
SIZE	2.2 to 2.5 inches.
HOST PLANTS	Willows.
FLIGHT	April to October.

50 · Weidemeyer's Admiral
Basilarchia weidemeyerii

RANGE	Higher mountains of the northern two thirds of the region.
SIZE	2.0 to 2.4 inches.
HOST PLANTS	Mostly aspen trees.
FLIGHT	June to August.

In summer, a hiker among high mountain aspens may well be accompanied by this species. Weidemeyer's admirals demonstrate the beauty of a limited number of colors in a butterfly pattern, with their black upper sides cut by a wide, white band across all wings. They perch on branches at eye level or above, along dirt roads or on creek edges. They rarely visit flowers but love a drink of water on a warm day.

To survive winter, the caterpillars hibernate after about three molts in a small, nest-like structure called a *hibernaculum*. This consists of a rolled-up leaf silked together so that the larva is parallel to the mid-rib of the leaf. This hibernaculum is simply a winter resting place, in which no metamorphosis occurs.

51 · California Sister
Adelpha bredowii

RANGE	Mountains and foothills throughout the region.
SIZE	2.5 to 2.9 inches.
HOST PLANTS	Oaks.
FLIGHT	Several broods, April to November.

This is one of the Southwest's most beautiful species. When California sisters perch, they may show the upper side of their wings of brown and white with orange tips or hold their wings together to reveal a lovely underside of brown, white, and powder blue.

Reluctant flower feeders, they spend much of their time patrolling up and down washes and across oak-covered hillsides and can often be seen gliding high, scarcely flapping their wings on their way between treetops. They love damp soil on hot days but are not willing subjects for close scrutiny. These butterflies have unusual tastes, reportedly feeding on excrement, fruit, and aphid honeydew. Females lay eggs singly on oak leaves, and adults winter in the larval stage.

52 · Hackberry Emperor
Asterocampa celtis

Hackberry emperors may occur wherever there are hackberry thickets along canyons and hillsides. Males perch high in trees and dart out at anything resembling a female, while females regularly take shelter deep in tangles of hackberry branches. You won't often see this species at flowers; it prefers mud, carrion, or runs of sap from trees, especially willows.

One of the two other southwestern species of hackberry butterflies, the empress Leilia (*Asterocampa leilia*), is limited to desert washes along the southern edge of the region. Where both species occur together, Leilias are more likely to perch on the ground while emperors perch on branches.

RANGE	Southern Nevada, south and east throughout much of the region.
SIZE	1.5 to 1.9 inches.
HOST PLANTS	Netleaf hackberries.
FLIGHT	May to September.

53 · Red Satyr *Megisto rubricata*

The satyrs are a small subgroup of the brush-foot family in various shades of brown. Their wings have veins that are swollen at the base and are thought to contain hearing organs.

Red satyrs are typical in that they do not nectar at flowers and have a bouncy, slow, erratic flight. They half open and close their wings when perched, exposing the mahogany-red patches for which they are named. Their undersides are tan with a few small eyespots.

In contrast with other satyrs, the red satyr often frequents hilltops or hillsides for both mate location and roosting at night.

RANGE	Oak-grassland in central Arizona and central New Mexico to west Texas.
SIZE	1.1 to 1.4 inches.
HOST PLANTS	Not documented, probably grasses.
FLIGHT	Mostly June to August.

54 · Mead's Wood-Nymph *Cercyonis meadii*

This is one of the more common species in piñon/juniper uplands throughout much of the Southwest. It extends up into pine forests and bounces across sagebrush flats when other species may be scarce. Its genus, in which the adults do take nectar, is represented by four species in the Southwest.

Mead's wood-nymphs may cluster at flowerheads such as yellow composites. The stigma, a dark brown patch on the front wings of males, carries scent scales to attract females during mating.

The caterpillars are green and tan and blend well with grass clumps and grass blades.

RANGE	Northwest Arizona, south and east to west Texas.
SIZE	1.4 to 1.6 inches.
HOST PLANTS	Undocumented, probably various grasses.
FLIGHT	July to September.

55 · Red-Bordered Satyr
Gyrocheilus patrobas

RANGE	Central Arizona and west-central New Mexico southward.
SIZE	1.8 to 2.1 inches.
HOST PLANTS	Grasses.
FLIGHT	September to October.

Anyone hiking in the mountains near the borders between Arizona, New Mexico, and Mexico in early autumn is likely to notice this satyr. It is an atypical satyr in that it is quite large in size and goes willingly to flowers. It is all the more noticed since it flies at a time when the Southwest is cooling off after the torrid summer and people are out enjoying themselves.

Red-bordered satyrs favor moist, steep canyons where they are fond of partial shade, puddle edges, and flowers such as star thistle. Their slow, bouncy, zigzag flight—often just above the grass tops—catches the eye, as does their midnight-brown color edged with a burnt orange hind wing patch. Adults are generally sedentary, as are other satyrs.

56 · Monarch
Danaus plexippus

The monarch is known throughout North America for its vast migrations and communal winter roostings, as well as its poisonous properties and resulting mimicry by the viceroy. The strength of its poison varies by individual, between sexes, and among populations, depending upon which milkweed has been ingested.

To send chemical messages to females, males have pronounced black spots, or *scent pouches*, on their hind wings and elongated hairs called *hair-pencils* on their abdomens.

Though not abundant in the Southwest, there are pockets of breeding monarchs where milkweeds are available. More people see monarchs during their 3,000-mile fall migration southward from Canada than at any other time of the year. The monarchs' strong flight, which averages around ten miles per hour, enables them to evade predators relatively easily.

RANGE	Throughout the region.
SIZE	3.3 to 3.7 inches.
HOST PLANTS	Milkweeds.
FLIGHT	Spring through fall, most commonly in the fall.

RANGE	Throughout the region, more commonly southward.
SIZE	2.4 to 2.6 inches, occasional dwarves.
HOST PLANTS	Milkweeds.
FLIGHT	March to November.

A smaller and duller desert counterpart of the monarch is the queen, which is also poisonous. It does not make the heroic journey that the monarch does, nor does it roost communally through winter in the thousands. Instead, the queen graces desert gardens and foothills with its presence most of the year, often in large numbers. Small numbers of male queens do roost on certain plants during the evenings, converting chemicals from these plants for use in mating.

In midsummer, the queen is one of the first butterflies to rouse in the early morning, sometimes being on the wing by 6 a.m. The chrysalids are gorgeous, a translucent, pale green with gold spots.

SKIPPER FAMILY
(Hesperiidae)

ORANGE SKIPPERLING

SKIPPERS ARE A WIDESPREAD FAMILY OF OVER THRITY-FIVE HUNDRED species, with their greatest development in the American tropics. Skippers in general are large-bodied, small-winged butterflies. As their name suggests, they have a powerful, rapid, jerky flight, the result of a thick, well-muscled thorax.

While most butterfly antennae are capped with a club, skippers' antennae have an *apiculus*, an extension of the antenna past the club that is curved or hooked downward.

For protection, many skipper caterpillars feed on the leaves of their foodplant at night, returning to their leaf tubes—silked-over, rolled leaves—by day.

In the Southwest, there are four main groups within the family: giant skippers (*Megathyminae*); herb, shrub, and tree skippers (*Pyrginae*); mimic skippers (*Pyrrhopyginae*); and branded skippers (*Hesperiinae*). More than 130 species of branded skippers occur in the United States, several dozen of them in the Southwest, and their identification can be quite difficult. In fact, some butterfly enthusiasts shun the skippers in general because of the difficulty in separating species.

58 · Silver-Spotted Skipper *Epargyreus clarus*

The silver-spotted skipper is one of the largest of the group. It is also one of the most distinctive, with a deep-brown tone broken on the upper side by golden spots on the front wings. On the underside there is a large, silvery-white spot on each hind wing that gives the species its name.

This is a butterfly of well-watered canyons and mountain slopes. In its preferred habitat, it is common at wet spots, fluttering above streamsides and then buzzing off with a very rapid flight. Males also favor bushes in clearings in the woods where they await passing females. As with most skippers, if a mating pair is disturbed during copulation, the female flies away carrying the male beneath her.

RANGE	Southern Nevada to Big Bend in the mountains.
SIZE	1.6 to 1.9 inches.
HOST PLANTS	Mostly tree legumes such as New Mexico locust.
FLIGHT	April to September, but mostly early summer.

59 · Dorantes Longtail *Urbanus dorantes*

This is the most common of a half dozen species of skippers with long tails that occur in the Southwest. During late summer and fall, small numbers of Dorantes enter the region to inhabit canyons with thick undergrowth, streamsides, and flowerbeds where they can find nectar sources such as lobelia and lantana.

They breed and become very common in some areas, only to have the adults wiped out by the first prolonged cold spell. Another species, the long-tailed skipper (*Urbanus proteus*), also turns up late in the year far north of its normal breeding range. Its body and the portion of the wings closest to the body are glossed in iridescent green.

RANGE	Southwestern Arizona to southwestern New Mexico.
SIZE	1.3 to 1.5 inches.
HOST PLANTS	A variety of herb legumes.
FLIGHT	July to October.

60 · Golden-Banded Skipper
Autochton cellus

The beautiful simplicity of this moderately sized brown butterfly, with its wide golden band across the fore wings, catches the eye of careful observers. The flash of gold is visible, even in flight, while the species cavorts along moist canyons. It also comes to flowers such as horsemint and indigobush, where it generally perches with the wings half opened. This species often perches on boughs of broad-leafed trees and shrubs at about eye level.

Golden-banded skippers are cyclical in abundance, being scarce some years and quite common in others. Look for this butterfly at mid-elevations in riparian zones through pine/oak woodland.

RANGE	Central Arizona and west central New Mexico southward; also Big Bend, Texas.
SIZE	1.3 to 1.6 inches.
HOST PLANTS	Herb legumes.
FLIGHT	June to August.

61 · Northern Cloudywing *Thorybes pylades*

This is the most common and widespread species of the medium-sized brown skippers with small, clear-to-white fore wing spots and mottling on the hind wing undersides. It perches with wings half open, a trait not shared by many of its look-alikes.

It is a butterfly of middle to high elevations, where it plays in broken sunlight and comes to damp soil. It will feed on a wide array of flowers such as loosestrife and locoweed and commonly perches on the ground.

A similar species, the acacia skipper (*Cogia hippalus*), occurs at lower elevations, usually in arroyos within desert hills and mountain foothills. It has white hind wing fringes, lands with its wings together, and can fly very rapidly.

RANGE	Throughout much of the region, always in the mountains.
SIZE	1.2 to 1.4 inches.
HOST PLANTS	Various herb legumes.
FLIGHT	May to August.

62 · Golden-Headed Scallopwing *Staphylus ceos*

Unless the casual observer follows this small, black, jerky-flighted butterfly beneath the canopy and under bushes, he or she might never get a good glimpse of the golden-headed scallopwing. When it perches, two things are noticeable: its wings are mostly opened and its head is a golden orange. Few other American butterflies have an orange head and palpi.

This is a lowland and middle-elevation skipper, usually associated with water. It comes to puddles and low-growing flowers, such as bidens. Adults fly faster than another similar species, the common sooty-wing (*Pholisora catullus*). The sooty-wing is found nearly across the country except for the lowest deserts, especially around disturbed soil, wastelands, and household gardens. They have white spotting on the front wings and lack the orange dusting around the head.

RANGE	Southern half of the region.
SIZE	.8 to 1.0 inch.
HOST PLANTS	Goosefoot and related plants.
FLIGHT	March to September, in several broods.

63 · Arizona Powdered Skipper *Systasea zampa*

What is most notable about this species is that the hind wing margins are wavy instead of smooth and round. That wavy edge, its moth-like look, plus the various shades of tan that comprise the pattern, all help to identify the Arizona powdered skipper. It is a species of desert washes and foothills, often on the wing during the hottest period of the day.

The Arizona powdered skipper comes to water but is most often found above creeks, away from water, on benches and flood plains. The males are very territorial, perching on twigs and hillsides with wings mostly opened and the tips drooping. Females are nearby, searching for plants on which they lay their eggs. Both sexes are fond of flowers such as fleabane and willow-leaf groundsel.

RANGE	Southern half of the region.
SIZE	.9 to 1.0 inch.
HOST PLANTS	Indian mallow and related plants.
FLIGHT	April to October, year-round in the hottest deserts.

64 · Sleepy Duskywing *Erynnis brizo*

Duskywings differ from other dark skippers in having heavily mottled front wings and immaculate, deep-brown hind wings. The dozen or so southwestern species of duskywings are mostly look-alikes. Experts can identify them by examining the male genitalia. Some, such as sleepy duskywings, have dark fringes at the ends of their hind wings while others have white fringes.

The sleepy duskywing is one of the earliest butterflies in spring, occurring throughout oak-rich forests when the first flowers bloom. Males come to water but are most often on hilltops, perching on, or very close to, the ground.

Many herb, shrub, and tree skippers, such as sleepy duskywings, can be sexually separated by a feature on the front wings: the forward edge in males has a *costal fold*, a flap on the vein like a small envelope that can be opened to reveal a tan interior with scent scales used for attracting mates. It is absent in females.

RANGE	All mountain ranges with stands of oaks.
SIZE	1.1 to 1.2 inches.
HOST PLANTS	Leaves or leaf buds of young oaks.
FLIGHT	March to May.

65 · Funereal Duskywing *Erynnis funeralis*

This is the most common duskywing in the Southwest, where it is at home from mountain meadows to desert flats. It is one of several with white fringes on the hind wings, but the front wings are longer and narrower than those of other duskywings.

Males perch at eye level on branches—on benches above streams and arroyos —and dart out at any movement. In late morning, they also perch on hilltop shrubs to await passing females. Both sexes visit garden flowers such as lantanas and zinnias and wildflowers such as rabbitbrush in desert washes.

RANGE	A wide range of habitats throughout the region.
SIZE	1.2 to 1.4 inches.
HOST PLANTS	Many plants in the legume family.
FLIGHT	March to October, year-round southward.

66 · Common Checkered-Skipper
Pyrgus communis

This butterfly is common along roadsides, in agricultural fields, and in desert washes. With its low, rapid flight, it could be mistaken for a moth. Males love to establish territories in dry streambeds and, if given time, will return to the same general area repeatedly. They perch on rocks, come to moist soil, and sip nectar avidly at a variety of flowers such as beggar's ticks and desert broom.

Since they are not territorial, the darker females are seen less frequently than males. While males are conspicuous in canyons, females are busy investigating suitable food plants for egg-laying sites. The genitalia of the common checkered-skipper appear in two configurations, suggesting that there may be two species involved in this complex.

RANGE	Throughout the region at all elevations.
SIZE	.8 to 1.0 inch.
HOST PLANTS	Mostly globe mallow.
FLIGHT	March to October northward, year-round in the deserts.

67· Orange Skipperling *Copaeodes aurantiacus*

When a hiker is passing between boulders up a deserted canyon and a little speck of an orange butterfly perches on a rock, it is most likely this tiniest of regularly occurring skippers in the Southwest. It is one of several mostly orange species called branded skippers that perch with hind wings opened nearly flat and fore wings mostly together. This odd position, often called the "jet plane" position, may be a means to regulate body temperature.

Orange skipperlings enjoy hot, dry canyons but are also occasionally found in city gardens and flower patches in the foothills. Their tiny size, coupled with a very rapid flight, make this species difficult to see and easy to overlook.

RANGE	Throughout the region, more commonly southward.
SIZE	.7 to .8 inch.
HOST PLANTS	Various grasses.
FLIGHT	March to October.

68· Fiery Skipper *Hylephila phyleus*

Of all the butterfly species in desert city gardens, fiery skippers are perhaps the most common. Since the caterpillars feed on Bermuda grass (the best lawn to survive scorching summers), many desert gardens harbor this species. Both sexes fly low over lawns, perch on adjacent shrubs, and come to almost any available nectar, such as lantanas and verbenas.

Away from towns, fiery skippers are scarce in spring but increase in abundance by late summer and fall, establishing themselves further northward with each successive brood.

Males are mostly orange with a few dark spots, while females are a more highly patterned mix of orange, tan, and dark brown. Both sexes have very short antennae.

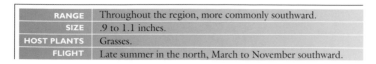

RANGE	Throughout the region, more commonly southward.
SIZE	.9 to 1.1 inches.
HOST PLANTS	Grasses.
FLIGHT	Late summer in the north, March to November southward.

69 · Pahaska Skipper *Hesperia pahaska*

One characteristic of male branded skippers is the presence of a *stigma* in males: a black dash, patch, or broken line on the upper surface of the front wings. A microscope reveals this to be a pocket filled with dusty, specialized scales of yellow, gray, or black, which are scented with pheromones used to attract mates.

Pahaska skippers have prominent stigmata that appear black but are actually filled with yellow sex scales. On the underside of their hind wings, they have a straight row of white dots. They are a grassland species of prairies, high deserts, and chaparral. Males are strong hilltoppers, while females visit flowers such as rabbitbrush and locoweed.

The green skipper (*Hesperia viridis*) is similar but has black rather than yellow sex scaling and a more concave row of white dots on the underside of its hind wings. Male green skippers do not hilltop. They range from eastern Arizona through New Mexico into western Texas.

RANGE	Much of the region outside the lowest deserts.
SIZE	.8 to 1.1 inches.
HOST PLANTS	Grasses.
FLIGHT	Early summer in the north, April to October southward.

70 · Taxiles Skipper *Poanes taxiles*

While hiking in the mountains at middle or high elevations, an observer might notice two quite different-looking skippers that are actually the same species. The taxiles skipper is an example of sexual dimorphism in butterflies. Male taxiles skippers are bright orange with a dark border around all wings, but the females are mostly brown with small amounts of orange and with dark, mottled hind wings underneath.

Adults are ardent visitors to such flowers as horsemint and thistle. Males perch on the ground and on branches in clearings in the forest to wait for passing females. On warm days, both sexes favor partial shade.

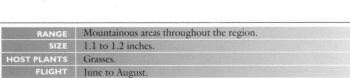

RANGE	Mountainous areas throughout the region.
SIZE	1.1 to 1.2 inches.
HOST PLANTS	Grasses.
FLIGHT	June to August.

GLOSSARY

androconia: specialized sex scales on adult male wings

apiculus: in skippers, the bent portion of the antennae beyond the club

basking: any of several positions used by adult butterflies to raise the body temperature

Batesian mimicry: a means of protection by an edible species in which it mimics the appearance of a poisonous species

chrysalis: a stage of metamorphosis between the larva and adult; a pupa

costal fold: a pocket on the leading edge of the fore wings of skippers containing specialized sex scales

falcate: sickle-shaped, usually pertaining to the shape of a pointed fore wing

hair pencils: clusters of hair-like scent scales used in courtship

hibernaculum: a winter larval nest

hilltopping: a means of mate location involving the summits of hills, used by males of many species

jet plane position: a perching position in skippers used as a means of thermoregulation

larva: (plural: larvae) the young of a butterfly; a caterpillar

long day-length: the period of time during the year when daylight hours are longer than nighttime hours

lunules: crescent-shaped spots on the wings

molt: to shed the larval skin or exoskeleton

osmeterium: an orange, foul-smelling organ behind the caterpillar's head, used to deter predators

oviposition: the laying of eggs, either singly or in groups

palpi: a paired organ on an adult butterfly's head, aiding in the sense of smell

pheromone: any chemical used to elicit a response in another butterfly, often used in attracting mates

puddle party: a congregation of butterfly individuals of one or more species at wet sand or mud

pupa: (plural: pupae) a mummy-like resting stage in metamorphosis between the larval and adult forms

scent pouch: a pocket on the wing of a butterfly containing sex scaling, used in courtship

seasonally dimorphic: the individual broods of a species differ in appearance based on the seasons

sexually dimorphic: the two sexes of a species differ considerably in outward appearance

short day-length: the period of time when daylight hours are shorter than nighttime hours

species: a basic unit of classification comprising all individuals of one type which are able to breed and produce healthy offspring

stigma: (plural: stigmata) any conspicuous patch of specialized scent scales on the wings

stink club: an organ on the abdomen of females, in some brush-footed butterflies, used in courtship

subspecies: a subgroup of a species that occupies a distinct geographic range

thermoregulate: the ability of a butterfly to alter its body temperature by changing its position or behavior

venation: the pattern of tubular supports on the wings, necessary for flight and used in separating butterfly families

SUGGESTED READING

Bailowitz, R. A. and J. P. Brock: *Butterflies of Southeastern Arizona*, Sonoran
    Arthropod Studies, Inc., Tucson 1991.

Brown, F. M., D. Eff, and B. Rotger: *Colorado Butterflies*, Denver Museum
    of Natural History Proceedings, Denver 1957.

Emmel, T. C. and J. F. Emmel: *The Butterflies of Southern California*,
    Natural History Museum of Los Angeles County, Scientific Series # 26,
    Los Angeles 1973.

Epple, A. O.: *A Field Guide to the Plants of Arizona*, LewAnn Publishing,
    Mesa, Arizona 1995.

Ferris, C. and F. M. Brown: *Butterflies of the Rocky Mountain States*,
    University of Oklahoma Press, Norman 1981.

Howe, W. E.: *The Butterflies of North America*, Doubleday, New York 1975.

Pyle, R. M. *The Audubon Society Field Guide to North American Butterflies*,
    Alfred A. Knopf, New York 1981.

Scott, J. A. *The Butterflies of North America*, Stanford University Press,
    Stanford, California 1986.

Tilden, J. W. and A. C. Smith. *A Field Guide to Western Butterflies*,
    Houghton Mifflin, Boston 1986.

RELATED ORGANIZATIONS

The Lepidopterists' Society
257 Common Street
Dedham, Massachusetts 02026

Xerces Society
4828 SE Hawthorne Blvd.
Portland, Oregon 97204

Lepidoptera Research Foundation, Inc.
9620 Heather Road
Beverly Hills, California 90210

Association for Tropical Lepidoptera
P. O. Box 141210
Gainesville, Florida 32614

Sonoran Arthropod Studies Institute
P. O. Box 5624
Tucson, Arizona 85703

North American Butterfly Association
4 Delaware Road
Morristown, New Jersey 07960

INDEX